W9-CUA-330

Looking for Holes in the Ceiling

Looking for Holes

in the Ceiling

Poems by Stephen Dunn

University of Massachusetts Press Amherst, 1974

To Lois;

and to Sam & Faith Toperoff

Copyrights and Acknowledgements
Abraxas for "Monologue on the Way Out" from *The Abraxas/5 Anthology.* Copyright © 1972 by
Abraxas. Antaeus for "Looking for a Rest Area." Copyright © 1972 by *Antaeus. Dacotah
Territory* for "Palominos," previously titled "Real Toads." Copyright © 1973 by *Dacotah Territory.
Hearse* for "An Ambulance Is Coming" and "Fat Man, Floating." Copyright © 1972 by *Hearse.
Kayak* for "If I Were in Charge of Epiphanies." Copyright © 1973 by *Kayak. The New Republic*
for "On Hearing the Airlines Will Use a Psychological Profile to Catch Potential Skyjackers," "To
the Upright," and "Teacher Answering Young Radicals." Reprinted by permission of *The New
Republic,* © 1972 (71) (70) Harrison-Blaine of New Jersey, Inc. *The New York Quarterly* for
"What" and "Poem." Reprinted by permission of *The New York Quarterly,* © 1971 by *The New
York Quarterly.* Ox Head Press for "The Rapist" from *Five Impersonations.* Copyright © 1971 by
Stephen Dunn. *Pebble* for "Among Blackberries." Copyright © 1972 by *Pebble. Poetry* for "Men in
Winter." Copyright © 1972 by *Poetry. Poetry Northwest* for "Dancing on Park Avenue," "How to
Be Happy: Another Memo to Myself," "Lakes: The Ocean Speaking," "Biography in the First
Person," "The Loss," and "Affirmation." Copyright © 1974, 1973, 1973, 1971, 1971, 1970 by
Poetry Northwest. Poetry Now for the ten poems "Sympathetic Magic." Copyright © 1974 by
Poetry Now. Shenandoah for "A Poem for Atheists," "Carrying On," and "A Man Waiting for It
to Stop." Copyright © 1972, 1972, 1971 by *Shenandoah,* reprinted from *Shenandoah:* The Washington
and Lee University Review with the permission of the Editor. *Southern Poetry Review* for "The
Rider." Copyright © 1973 by *Southern Poetry Review. Three Rivers Poetry Journal* for "Day and
Night Handball." Copyright © 1973 by Three Rivers Press. Winthrop Publishers, Inc. for "At
Every Gas Station There Are Mechanics" from *New Voices in American Poetry.* Copyright © 1973
by Stephen Dunn.

Contents

I. A Man Waiting for It to Stop

II. Sympathetic Magic

III. Looking for Holes in The Ceiling

IV. Carrying On

I. A Man Waiting for it to Stop

What

What starts things

are the accidents behind the eyes
touched off by, say, the missing cheekbone
of a woman who might have been beautiful

it is thinking about
your transplanted life-line going places
in someone else's palm, or the suicidal games
your mind plays with the edge
of old wounds, or something
you couldn't share with your lover

there are no endings

people die between birthdays and go on for years;
what stops things for a moment
are the words you've found for the last bit of light
you think there is

The Rapist

I am the man crouched behind a bush
sitting at his desk.
I will never be caught. All my victims
have a way of disappearing.
No matter what sex you are,
you will be next.
You would sit next to me
at a concert performed in the woods.
If I looked at you in the subway
you would not shift your eyes.
I am small, deceptive
like this poem
that is already inside you.

In Certain Places at Certain Times
There Can Be More of You

1

Once crossing a plush street
in Caracas, I stepped into South America:
shacks falling over, urchins sucking
empty bottles. Later that night
I found a pair of shoes
under a streetlamp, their insides still warm.

I remember thinking there's a cat loose
somewhere: a man in his socks.
Or worse, something has lifted a man
out of his shoes.

When I looked to myself
for what to do,
there were too many masks.
They each fit tightly around my face.

I started to walk.
Nearby, someone in a Fiat
slammed his brakes.
My body began to speak
its silent bloodrush,
the native tongue, look out
for yourself.

2

Months later, driving from New York
to Pennsylvania,
I passed the slag heaps
outside Scranton
and eighty miles later
The Bean Soup Festival in McClure.

I had crossed a street.

There was no one with me,
and when I leaned over and looked
at myself in the rear-view mirror
all the faces had different expressions.

This is a crazy country, I thought.
I can afford them.

A Man Waiting For It to Stop

It is due to come soon.

There is security at bus stops—
he has watched headlights find their way
    to him,
no one has discovered the sweat on the nickels
he holds, how open doors make him feel.

Behind his eyes are drum majorettes
walking toward him with their hands full
of other boys, and wheat-faced girls
    he can taste
as they come out of rooms, past him,
and the Puerto Rican whore who leads him
past her parents with cobalt, unbudged eyes
she is there, too
as he empties his pockets into her mouth.

Nothing can happen, now,
if he waits in the right places, if he moves
without moving himself.

When it comes it will take him to the corner
of Groton and Sixty-eighth, the last stop,
    the neighborhood
where he never grew up, and must return to.

He can see his mother's friends with vacancies
for lovers in their open, blue faces
the alert nipple beneath the first torn blouse.

It is simple, once he gets there, to get back.
And back again.

Dancing on Park Avenue

"Things are getting so bad that people
are committing celibacy in the streets."
  —From a freshman composition

It doesn't matter,
but when the sun comes up
who can say I didn't bring it?
I am dancing on Park Avenue.

A man closes his lids
on my entire body.
Taxi drivers scream
"Faggot" through their side vents.

The woman in me is ecstatic.
She has never heard such praise.
"Fruit!" someone else yells;
I have kept her hidden too long.

There are no words that can touch
my manhood. I am the cock
of the sleeping fifties,
doing the flamenco.

I have attracted a small crowd.
I ask them, who can separate the dancer
from the dance? They are calling the police
in their heads. I ask them to reach out

for the missing rib of their existence.
I ask them for their bodies,
for the beautiful numbed beast
of their childhood. They are

silent. They are not really here.
The wind is blowing empty cartons

8

down the street.
I put away my breasts

and walk home dodging cracks
in the sidewalk.
It is still dark.
No one is awake.

Poem

*"What has become perfect, all
that is ripe—wants to die."*
—Nietzsche

When the sun goes down
women who have loosened celebrations
listen for the sound of keys—
and boys, mad with their age and stuck
in small skins, imagine their bones
the chassis for some Buick.
Animals find themselves crouching in woods,
men behind their last idea.

Soon the manual for living after dark
starts to fall from the mouths of mothers.
Things settle down,
get so quiet you could hear a pin
enter the heart of a doll.
And here and there people are found indoors
wondering if the moth, wild inside a lampshade,
is ecstatic.

The Loss

Even the tips of their fingers
seem to be retreating

their eyes appear ransacked
of what was wide and American

if you had told them
that history is a small circle, that

toward everybody
a line is moving

they would have laughed
they were the kind

who lose their teeth
when a jack-in-the-box

comes out swinging
though now everything is clear, clear

as an old telegram.
Some are sitting by themselves

some have folded their hands
as far removed from prayer

as poker players who have found themselves
with nothing

Teacher Answering Young Radicals

Given the choice of blowing up the Empire
State Building or a department store, he said balloons
took his breath away, too.

Then he took the wind in his fist
and let it out like a butterfly,
to show what power was.

When no one understood,
he let himself go
and they followed the simple flight of his mind

flower to flower. Then he raised his fist
into a hammer and slammed it to the table,
to show what weakness was.

He had them,
and could have lifted them with his voice
to where blood gets thin as air

and honest rage suffocates in the throat.
He told them instead about his fist,
the dull pain up his arm, turning warm.

To the Upright

Excuse me. Do not speak of nerves
gone dead, nor of pain

with no hurt inside it.
Perhaps

men with bad knees
shouldn't be expected

to do deep things, or move
to fix whatever in the world

is wrong. Theirs was a youth
without spring, of endless

drag bunts they dreamed
of beating to first.

So what if their knees stick out
in every conversation.

So the natural crack of bones
as they rise from low chairs

sends them into the hollow
of old trumpets. So what.

You see through them with an eye,
perhaps, that has never turned in

where the water collects
around your heart.

At Every Gas Station There Are Mechanics

Around them my cleanliness stinks.
I smell it. And so do they.
I always want to tell them I used to box,
and change tires, and eat heroes.
It is my hands hanging out
of my sleeves like white gloves.
It is what I've not done, and do not know.
If they mention the differential
I pay whatever price. When
they tell me what's wrong beneath my hood
I nod, and become meek.
If they were to say I could not
have my car back, that it was theirs,
I would say thank you, you must be right.
And then I would walk home,
and create an accident.

An Ambulance Is Coming

A glove is lying on the curb.
There is a hand in it,
and there is an arm
reaching into that hand, bonelocked
at the wrist, and a body
jammed onto that arm, a body
lying on the sidewalk. Yet this
is not a simple tale
of a man dipping his body
into his glove in order to pick it up.
The body is unconscious, it has been
coldcocked by a fist
which has sped away in the pocket
of another man, its knuckles bleeding
in the dark, the blood seeping
through a hole in the pocket, down
the leg of the man, into his socks
as if his knees were in tears.
And the siren of the ambulance
beats the ambulance to the man
on the curb, stirs him
and when the ambulance comes, he's gone.
And blocks away the police arrest
a man for looking like a man
who might carry a fist in his pocket.
They want to take away his shoes,
and empty his life into a little hole.
But he has connections. This is
a story about things like that.

Fat Man, Floating

He is thinking
fish move beneath him
like the quick slender arms
of ballerinas. He is thinking
of the names he resembles.

Small waves drag their tongues
across his body, and children
in rowboats throw make-believe
harpoons. They enter his ears,
and never come out. He rolls

and fish look up at his face
as if it were a huge, unlit moon.
They swim into his eyes, touch
his mind and leave so silently
he would like to follow them

to the bottom, kick his way
under a rock, and live
without the kind of breath
people shape into knives.
But he just floats, rolls

on his back
and stops the sun with his hand.
His palm predicts a life as far
as his wrist. A gull swoops low
to see what he is.

Monologue on the Way Out

I've been places where the laughter is as contagious
      as a yawn,
I've been through windows, and other ordeals.
One summer I took a switchblade to every ceiling I knew.

There are reasons for leaving dinner parties in the middle
      of soup.

Let's just say I know what rugs think of housewives who shake
the footsteps from them, and call it cleaning.
Let's just say I know why midgets think of buying horses
and killing themselves in parks that have no statues.

I am the bomb inside a stone.
I am a tongue surrounded by teeth.

There are reasons why floors suddenly splinter and give in.
Let's just say I've been people who knew these things.

II. Sympathetic Magic

1. Adopting a Boy

Wear a loose garment.
Take the boy
and push him through your clothes.
He is your son now.
The law is strict,
if you pretend to give birth
the child is really yours.
In public, so everyone knows,
let him crawl
between your legs from behind.
When he comes through stroke him
with leaves from an elm.
Tie him to you.
After you have waddled together
back and forth,
everyone will nod.
The oldest woman will cry out.
Your breasts will fill with milk.

2. Making a Storm

After childbirth, go outdoors.
Fill your mouth with air.
On the way back to the house
blow it out: a storm will start.
If your child is a boy
there are ways to stop the storm.
You must find a stone
lodged in the belly of a fish.
Wind horsehair around it.
Tie it to a stick, then wave the stick
until the clouds become obedient
and move on.
If your child is a girl
adorn your breasts
with white circles and crescents.
Just make yourself lovely.
There is nothing you can do
about the storm.

3. Fighting

Before a battle do not eat hedgehog.
That animal curls up into a ball
when it's alarmed.
And do not make soup
from the bones of an ox.
It's weak in the knees
and you'll be unable to run.
It is good, though, to keep the hair
of a red bull in your pocket.
And the sharp bones of a fish
near the weapon you'll carry.
Try to make yourself believe
as the knife dries
the wound heals.

4. Hunting

If you are going to hunt elephants
don't let your wife cut her hair.
The elephant will
break through the ropes.
Also do not let her oil herself.
The elephant will slip through.
She must scatter popcorn
on the verandah every morning
so that you will be agile.
If you get hurt, it is her fault.
She has been unfaithful.
The elephant will knock over trees
to get to you.

5. Infertility

When it gets dark
strip yourself of all garments
and lie down
on the grave of twins.
After you've said
"Springs of water, rise,
myself into myself,"
cover it with candles,
nosegays and ribbons.
You'll want to go home then.
If your husband is asleep
rub his penis with cocoanut oil
and believe
you've done everything you could.
Pass the burden, lovingly, to him.

6. Cheating the Wizard

Understand this:
the wizard does not care
whose soul he takes.
He is a wizard, he just likes the feel
of it in his palms.
He thinks: the animal inside the animal,
the man inside the man,
and goes crazy with desire.
And don't forget your shadow
is your soul looking for perspective.
Be careful of your shadow.
If a hyena steps on it
you will lose all speech.
The hyena/the wizard.
When your children are sleeping
do not wake them too quickly.
Their souls get away
and need time to return.
Yes, get away with the wizard.
You need a fish hook soaked in brine
to get back a lost soul.
Walk into a dark room
with the fish hook in front of you.
Move it from side to side.
There'll be a moment
of the most delicate contact,
and you'll feel whole.
Or whatever it was you lost
wasn't your soul,
there'll be nothing,
and there's no telling how long
you'll grope in the dark.

7. Lovers

To keep the one you want
dig up a footprint of hers
and put it in a flowerpot.
Then plant a marigold, the flower
that doesn't fade.
And love her.
If she's distant now
it's for a reason beyond control.
So don't tamper with the impressions
left by her body when
for the last time
she leaves your bed.
Just smooth them out
and forget her.
Who is not vulnerable
to a stronger magic (the
broken glass, the bullets
in a yawn),
the terrible power of the one
less in love.

8. Chipping Away at Death

Build a man of straw and rags
and give him a foolish, battered hat.
There, he is you in old age.
Then when the swallows come
from the south, dig up the brandy
you buried the year before.
Taste it. It will taste like
the musk of a religion
you gave up
for the sweeter taste of women.
Cover your straw man with it.
Light a match.
If you want to throw chestnuts
into the fire and sing
squalid songs as he burns, do so.
You are making sure none of this
will ever happen,
making sure this is one death
you will not suffer.

9. Isolation

Look for a place lightning has struck
leaving a cleft in a tree,
and locate the stone which is
an amulet hidden there.
After a great loss
this is where to come.
This is the isolation that has
waited for you like a chrysalis
all these years.
Sit crosslegged and do not speak.
Warm the stone in your hands.
Soon you will feel the pain
grow wings and enter
the tree like dead lightning.
Do not move.
You have found your spot, the place
we all pass many times
until we live long enough to see it.

10. Traveling

If you travel alone, hitchhiking,
sleeping in woods,
make a cathedral of the moonlight
that reaches you, and lie down in it.
Shake a box of nails
at the night sounds
for there is comfort in your own noise.
And say out loud:
somebody at sunrise be distraught
   for love of me,
somebody at sunset call my name
There will soon be company.
But if the moon clouds over
you have to live with disapproval.
You are a traveler,
you know the open, hostile smiles
of those stuck in their lives.
Make a fire.
If the Devil sits down, offering companionship,
tell him you've always admired
his magnificent, false moves.
Then recite the list
of what you've learned to do without.
It is stronger than prayer.

III. Looking for Holes in the Ceiling

Biography in the First Person

This is not the way I am.
Really, I am much taller in person,
the hairline I conceal reaches back
to my grandfather, and the shyness my wife
will not believe in has always been why
I was bold on first dates. All my uncles
were detectives. My father a crack salesman.
I've saved his pins, the small acclamations
I used to show my friends. And the billyclub
I keep by my bed was his, too; an heirloom.
I am somewhat older than you can tell.
The early deaths have decomposed
behind my eyes, leaving lines apparently caused
by smiling. My voice still reflects the time
I believed in prayer as a way of getting
what I wanted. I am none of my clothes.
My poems are approximately true.
The games I play and how I play them
are the arrows you should follow: they'll take you
to the enormous body of a child. It is not
that simple. At parties I have been known to remove
from the bookshelf the kind of book
that goes best with my beard.
My habits in bed are so perverse they differentiate me
from no one. And I prefer soda, the bubbles just after
it's opened, to anyone who just lies there. Be careful:
I would like to make you believe in me.
When I come home at night after teaching myself
to students, I want to search the phone book
for their numbers, call them, and pick their brains.
Oh, I am much less flamboyant than this.
If you ever meet me, I'll be the one with the lapel
            full of carnations.

If I Were in Charge of Epiphanies

small significant bumps would appear on your skin
and the accidental laughter in church would begin
to form a pattern, say, in the Dakotas.

Soon you would look to yourself for miracles.
People south of Bismarck would start to wonder
why women come out of supermarkets totally satisfied.

Around your enormous navel small hairs
would spring up and spell words
you were never able to say.
Van Gogh would appear in wheatfields with a basket
of new eyes.

You would come to me with questions.
A young girl in Kansas would swear to her parents
(and later to the world) that an agnostic revealed
himself to her behind a huge rock.

You would feel something turn deep inside you,
like a key.
All the bramble in Northern Texas would be accused
of immolation.

Living in Someone Else's House

The house we never built for ourselves
begins to surround us,
its foundations smelling
like old breath

like what lies around too long
in the pit
of the stomach.
We are unable to sleep

in these houses made by someone else,
these furnished rooms we come to,
these outposts in the valleys
of our expectations.

Where we would have windows
there are portraits of landscapes,
or portraits of windows
opening out onto landscapes

and the doors open too easily
into the sunshine,
which is just a billboard
in the neighborhoods of the poor.

In these houses
the ceilings are so perfect
there's not a single invitation
to an angel,

our hopes smack into them
and we are afraid to move.
We find ourselves
stuck to the floor,

dynamite in our hands
and our hands waiting
for the orders
we wish we could give them.

Decisions to Disappear

In the dream of my death
I am a shimmering, empty space; gone
yet somehow noticed.
Awake, I think of a photograph—
a woman with her arm draped
around thin air, *thin air*;
what a desire I have
to be that suggestive.
I often imagine myself absent,
on the tip of somebody's tongue.
Sometimes I make phone calls
to old lovers,
inventing myself again.

But then there are those nights
when someone has yawned
and made me invisible, which lead
to more serious disappearances
and other nights of drifting,
unrecognized, through the house.
God knows I've tried
to keep these decisions for myself.
Yet how easily the cloak I wear
leaves my shoulders, lifted by hands
that have nothing to do with me,
and I stand there
conspicuous as silence.

Palominos

In Manhattan, when the flies gathered
around the mouth of a wino, sticking
in the muscatel on his chin and dying,
I was feeding a palomino—
I have always been feeding a palomino;
when the tanks rolled in Athens
the palomino I needed for departure
finished the last of my apples,
in Spain when the Guardia raised his machine gun
I was feeding a palomino though my hands appeared
to be reaching into the air;
I could do it in my sleep
in a room half the size of a palomino
if I had to, it's a luxury
the way escaping through the window
of an office that never existed
is a luxury only men who feed palominos really know.
Can you understand?
Beneath my shirt where my heart once was
a small orphanned palomino moans
when women slip their hands inside; this
is his only food, and he hasn't been eating well lately.
Once in Aruba the dark hands of a prostitute
turned him into a stallion,
and in Denver one cold afternoon I tried
feeding him with my own hands, but he knew
the difference, bit at my shirt, bit at
my invisible palomino monogram, left me naked,
open to ridicule.
But I would never stop feeding palominos;
at dinner last night, in that peculiar silence
that follows burnt vegetables, overdone beef,
several palominos licked my fingers
beneath the table. One of them was pregnant,
she ate like a horse, and I climbed on her
and she took me for a ride where other palominos were
and the dinner became meaningless

and I loved my wife.
That is what palominos will do for you
if you feed them, it is their special dignity,
their hunger for the loose hay we all have
lying around.
Right now there are carrots in my pocket
that look like palominos would love them
if the occasion ever arises,
but here on this farm outside of Syracuse
things are so quiet, the summer is practically over
and there is a palomino out back
who is so real I must feed her every day,
happy or not. She is very beautiful.
But she cannot be counted on in emergencies.

A Poem for Atheists

I drill a hole in my ceiling,
hoping for the best.
It is a hole in the floor
when I go upstairs and that alone
is something,
but not very much.
Friends come over. They urge me
to fix it, to make it appear
as if nothing had happened,
and that is very funny.
So I draw eyelashes around it
Oh, it is a joke people say
but they don't understand
it is not a joke, too.
Upstairs, I get on my stomach
and downstairs I stand on
my own two feet watching it
and looking through it,
hoping for the best.
I give it a name
to distinguish it from others
Roberta I call it
but that is hardly the last word
there are names now
for craters in the moon
for the gaps in my resume
for oblivion.
So next to it with great strokes
I design the hieroglyphic for prudes
to do
what my face alone could never accomplish.
Gradually, I forget about it
only a spider now and then
reminds me
of what foresight I had
though there have been no messages
not even a pole,
nor a fireman.

40

Thanksgiving:
Getting Together with Parents

*"Someone with no invisible means
of support."*
—Oscar Levant's definition
of an atheist

The table is set.
The names assigned.
Father is the candlestick
in the simple holder.
Mother, omnipresent,
a matrix of air
all around us.
My wife has said
"Now that everybody's dead
we will not live without them."
The turkey is served,
stuffed and garnished.
Potatoes follow, peas,
the works.
When it is time for prayer
we light the candle,
we breathe in,
we say hello and thanks.

Looking for a Rest Area

I've been driving for hours,
it seems like all my life.
The wheel has become familiar,
I turn it

every so often to avoid the end
of my life, but I'm never sure
it doesn't turn me
by its roundness, as women have

by the space inside them.
What I'm looking for
is a rest area, some place where
the old valentine inside my shirt

can stop contriving romances,
where I can climb out of the thing
that has taken me this far
and stretch myself.

It is dusk, Nebraska,
the only bright lights in this entire state
put their fists in my eyes
as they pass me.

Oh, how easily I can be dazzled—
where is the sign
that will free me, if only for moments,
I keep asking.

Men in Winter

All winter we stayed in, making light
of the day, watching the clouds become
elephants, replicas of Italy, beards.
We called it trivial, what was outside
of us. It was so much fun.

When the nights came with their villainous
capes, we said what a bad movie
we live in, and wondered who was
to be saved this time, ha ha,
and weren't the clouds low these days,

like aristocrats. It was a way
of passing time. We believed each of us
had a summer inside him, several deserted
beaches, a cove. When Spring came,
we'd had so much of ourselves we said *who cares*

and opened our doors like mad sailors
in a submarine, fathoms from this world.

The Rider

It is with me, that falling star
that fell halfway down
to Echo, Minnesota. I saw it

last night from the highway,
from a bucket seat,
a familiar wheel of comfort.

It fell fast and then stopped
the way a man falls in his dreams,
a spectacular hint of destruction

opening his eyes.

Who will believe me
if I insist
that a large man was riding it,

and the shell of a body
drove my car home into the vacancies
of garage and self,

without mishap, or a single regret?

IV. Carrying On

811.54

813.5

PLEASE ORDER FROM MIDWEST LIBRARY SERVICE
CATALOGING IN PUBLICATION 11/97

Brooker, Paul.
    Defiant dictatorships : communist and Middle-Eastern dicta-
torships in a democratic age / Paul Brooker. — New York : New
York University Press, 1997.
    p.   cm.
    Includes bibliographical references and index.
    ISBN 0-8147-1311-4

1. History, Modern—1945-   . 2. Dictatorship.   I. Title.

D445.B765   1997b   909.82—dc21   97-15332
                                              AACR 2   MARC CIP 11/97

Library of Congress

Day and Night Handball

I think of corner shots, the ball
hitting and dying like a butterfly
on a windshield, shots so fine
and perverse they begin to live

alongside weekends of sex
in your memory. I think of serves
delivered deep to the left hand,
the ball sliding off the side wall

into the blindnesses of one's body,
and diving returns that are impossible
except on days when your body is all
rubber bands and dreams

unfulfilled since childhood.
I think of a hand slicing the face
of a ball, so much english
that it comes back drunk

to your opponent who doesn't have
enough hands to hit it,
who hits it anyway, who makes you think
of "God!" and "Goddamn!", the pleasure

of falling to your knees
for what is superb, better than you.
But it's position I think of most,
the easy slam and victory

because you have a sense of yourself
and the court, the sense that old men
gone in the knees have,
one step in place of five,

finesse in place of power,
and all the time
the four walls around you
creating the hardship, the infinite variety.

On Hearing the Airlines Will Use
a Psychological Profile
to Catch Potential Skyjackers

They will catch me
as sure as the check-out girls
in every Woolworths have caught me, the badge
of my imagined theft shining in their eyes.

I will be approaching the ticket counter
and knowing myself, myselves,
will effect the nonchalance of a baron.
That is what they'll be looking for.

I'll say "Certainly is nice that the
airlines are taking these precautions,"
and the man behind the counter
will press a secret button,

there'll be a hand on my shoulder
(this will have happened before in a dream),
and in a back room they'll ask me
"Why were you going to do it?"

I'll say "You wouldn't believe
I just wanted to get to Cleveland?"
"No," they'll say.
So I'll tell them everything,

the plot to get the Pulitzer Prize
in exchange for the airplane,
the bomb in my pencil,
heroin in the heel of my boot.

Inevitably, it'll be downtown for booking,
newsmen pumping me for deprivation
during childhood,
the essential cause.

"There is no one cause for any human act,"
I'll tell them, thinking *finally*,
a chance to let the public in
on the themes of great literature.

And on and on, celebrating myself, offering
no resistance, assuming what they assume,
knowing, in a sense, there is no such thing
as the wrong man.

The Outlaw

If a cowboy wears a star
he's a sheriff.
What is he if he wears
a moon?
—from a three-year-old

———————————

He doesn't know how the switchblade
with his initials got where it did,

or, later, how that strange note left his hand
and made the teller press a button.

If you would ask him, he'd say
he was tired and sat down next to,

not behind, that bush at midnight;
that the check he wished to deposit

was in the pants he didn't step into,
for reasons he doesn't understand, that morning.

These are old stories, which the cops
with their pretty badges have heard

a thousand times. They slap the guy
around, or send in a shrink to work

his parents over. No one asks him
about his eyes, so open, as if fixed

on something large and sexual,
or the cool, seminal breeze he feels

inside his shirt. He's the only one in the room
who notices an irregular, thin line

like a boundary between countries
hanging between himself and the others.

When he mentions it, an ancient fist
rockets his head back.

He stares into the naked lightbulb
above the hard chair he's in,

and does not know why he smiles
or why they hover around him with their wild eyes.

Carrying On

Here, on the landscape between wishes
and preposterous conclusions, leaves
early in October anticipate their own death
   and rainbows
sometimes appear in the sky like smiles
from men who've just exercised their power.
When I'm not looking the clock goes on
   and on,
and temptation slips in, slowly,
like the season's last fly. I want to write
notes to eleven-year-old girls who might
     grow up
to love me. I want to ask madmen why I feel
if I were to walk into an opening anywhere
the bones in my nose would be crushed
   by the invisible glass.
I don't. I return to what's around me, birds
that seem too nervous to fly, rocks
as aimless as lost knuckles. When people visit
   I open
the red wine and ask if words make anything happen,
or what adults should put beneath
their pillows to make the mornings exciting.
   They are drunk
when they leave, their thin teeth are blue,
nothing they have said for hours
has made any sense. I feel so superior
   that I dash off
a dozen wry, complex sentences
to the unattainable this, the unattainable that,
asking them who they think they are. It works;
   for days I'm able
to pull rabbits out of the thinnest afternoons.
And move. And write. And keep it going
until it stops.

Among Blackberries

Off the ocean road in Montauk
blackberries grow conspicuous and wild
as young girls who suspect they'll die soon.
To pick them no excuse is necessary,
there's a narrow path toads leap across
and from it I reach to either side,
taking what I want.
All the snakes are imaginary.
They are the price, here, it seems.
The berries taste so good I sense
some poison,
some middleman gone without,
his children dying of old Porsches.
My hands are stained.

Sometimes I just continue to the beach,
showing the blackberries my mouth
as I pass, tempting them, imagining
if they stretched themselves toward me
it could be said:
they were the beautiful jailbait
who flashed something as I passed,
it wasn't my fault.
There's no easy way, though.
It has taken weeks to memorize the poison ivy,
and sometimes in among the vines
wood ticks climb on to my skin, dig
themselves a place, and will not die.

Affirmation

The young boys roll down the hill, laughing
like crickets. The grass submits
to them. They take its color
on their white backs. At the bottom,
enthralled with their bodies, their dizziness,
they look up at their mother
who has imagined they have just tumbled
from her womb
into a world less dark. She applauds.
They play dead
as stones, then suddenly burst into boys
once more, running up that long slope
to where they began.
Beneath a tree, stretched out with my dog,
something I used to have—a wish, perhaps,
comes back.

Lakes: The Ocean Speaking

The first thing you notice
is their lack of shoulders,
and you recall a woman
whose lip would occasionally tremble,
and another who needed something
as swift as perhaps the wind
to move her. Then you observe
a certain deficiency of spirit,
the ease with which they allow
fishermen to take all their secrets.
And, everywhere, the unrocked boats.
You note that nothing maniacal
seems to rule them, neither God
nor Devil, and their record of catastrophe
is marred by leg cramps and carelessness.
You notice, though, how much better
you can see yourself in them,
how, if you swim in them and drown,
there is only yourself to blame.
And how their quietness seems
so righteous, yet so engaging.
Gradually you sense a reluctance
to say anything final about how deep
they are, or if they are beautiful—
a feeling that you must wake up
next to them many mornings
and become part of their worst moments,
their imperceptible breathing.

How to Be Happy: Another Memo to Myself

You start with your own body
then move outward, but not too far.
Never try to please a city, for example.
Nor will the easy intimacy
in small towns ever satisfy that need
you have only whispered in the dark.
A woman is a beginning.
She need not be pretty, but must know
how to make her own ceilings
out of all that is beautiful in her.
Together you must love to exchange
gifts in the night, and agree
on the superfluity of ribbons,
the fine violence of breaking out
of yourselves. No matter,
it is doubtful she will be enough for you,
or you for her. You must have friends
of both sexes. When you get together
you must feel everyone has brought
his fierce privacy with him
and is ready to share it. Prepare
yourself though to keep something back;
there is a center in you
you are simply a comedian
without. Beyond this, it is advisable
to have a skill. Learn how to make something:
food, a shoe box, a nice day.
That should be enough.
Remember, finally, there are few pleasures
that aren't as local as your fingertips.
Never go to Europe for a cathedral.
In large groups, create a corner
in the middle of a room.